ABHINANDAN PATIL

Essential Knowledge for Computer Scientists and Engineers

Copyright © 2023 by Abhinandan Patil

All rights reserved. No part of this publication may be reproduced, stored or transmitted in any form or by any means, electronic, mechanical, photocopying, recording, scanning, or otherwise without written permission from the publisher. It is illegal to copy this book, post it to a website, or distribute it by any other means without permission.

Abhinandan Patil asserts the moral right to be identified as the author of this work.

Abhinandan Patil has no responsibility for the persistence or accuracy of URLs for external or third-party Internet Websites referred to in this publication and does not guarantee that any content on such Websites is, or will remain, accurate or appropriate.

Designations used by companies to distinguish their products are often claimed as trademarks. All brand names and product names used in this book and on its cover are trade names, service marks, trademarks and registered trademarks of their respective owners. The publishers and the book are not associated with any product or vendor mentioned in this book. None of the companies referenced within the book have endorsed the book.

First edition

This book was professionally typeset on Reedsy.
Find out more at reedsy.com

Contents

Dedication	vii
Preface	viii
Acknowledgment	ix
About Me	x

I Mathematics for Computer Scientists and Engineers

1 Mathematics for Computer Scientists and Engineers	3
2 Probability and Statistics for Engineers and Scientists	5

II Electronics for Computer Scientists and Engineers

3 Analog and Digital Circuits	9
4 Micro Controllers	10
5 Computer Architecture	11

III Programming Languages for Computer Scientists and Engineers

6 C, C++, GoLang and Rust	15
7 Python, Java, Kotlin, JavaScript, HTML5 and CSS3	16

IV Software Engineering

8 Software Engineering	19
9 Software Architecture and Design	20

10 Software Testing   21

V   Scientific Software

11 Scientific Software   25

VI Data Structures and Algorithm

12 Data Structures and Algorithms   29

VII Computer Networking

13 Computer Networking   33

VIII Operating System

14 Operating System   37

IX Finite Automata, Formal Languages and Logic in Computer Science

15 Finite Automata, Formal Languages and Logic in Computer...   41

X   Utilities for Computer Scientists and Engineers

XI Web Technologies

16 Web Technologies   47

XII Data Bases

17 Data bases   51

XIII Productivity Software Such as Office Suites

18 Productivity Software   55

XIV Artificial Intelligence

19 Artificial Intelligence   59
20 Machine Learning and Deep Learning   60
21 Natural Language Processing   62
22 Re-Inforcement Learning.   63
23 Few Good Teachers of Practical AI/ML/DL/RL   64

XV Data Science

24 Data Analytics and Data Science   67

XVI Digital Transformation Technologies

25 Digital Transformation Technologies   71
    Cloud: 71
    (I)IoT: 72
    AI: 73
    Block Chain: 73
    Communication Technologies: 73
    Security: 74

XVII Quantum Computing

26 Quantum Computing   77

XVIII Sun Rise Sectors and Role of Computer Scientists
and Engineers in Sun Rise Sectors

27 Sunrise Sectors   81

XIX Robotics

28 Robotics   85

XX Security

XXI Reference Material

XXII Non Technical Knowledge aka. Intangible Traits

Conclusion   93

Dedication

Dedicated to my Family, Well-wishers and Teachers

Preface

The targeted readers of this book are mostly budding computer scientists and engineers. Undergraduates of computer science and engineering. This book should serve as a starting point for them and should give them a broad picture of what is what. The author makes an attempt to document his own understanding in this book. The book should serve as a reference book of reference books. This book contains curated pointers for further study. The book intentionally touches on too many topics while not getting into deep details of the topics. That is intentional. The author keeps the Text minimal. The motto is not to reinvent the wheel and make maximum use of already published authoritative content. At places, I might reuse text from my own Book "Essential Skills for Software Engineers". This Book can be used as a reference book while designing the syllabus at Universities for Computer Science and Engineering.

Acknowledgment

The author acknowledges Reedsy for great documentation software. Microsoft is acknowledged for providing a great host Windows operating system platform and Edge browser. The author also acknowledges all other software used for creating this work. Dell is acknowledged for its great hardware.

About Me

I am a resource person with 20 years of experience with exposure to both Industry and Academia with vast software Industry experience and a proven track record in publications. Quantitatively, 14 years of Industry experience, 14 research paper publications, 15 book publications, 5.5 years of Research experience, and 1 year of faculty experience. Vidwan score of 8.8, Academic/Research score of 505 as per UGC API calculator 2018 Table 2 for Engineering.

- Senior Member of IEEE (Member Id: 92139708)
- Google Scholar: https://scholar.google.com/citations?user=GV2y6GYAAAAJ
- LinkedIn: https://www.linkedin.com/in/Abhinandan-h-patil
- Vidwan: https://vidwan.inflibnet.ac.in/profile/391153
- ORC-ID: Published 0000-0002-8425-1493
- Personal Website: http://abhinandanhpatil.info
- Teacher with educational content on YouTube.
- Industrial Certifications: ISTQB-CTAL-TM, CSM, SMIEEE, PMI-PMP, UGC-NET, Indian Achiever 2021-2022

I am an accomplished Author, Technologist, Researcher and Educator.

My area of Research is Software Engineering, Software Testing, Emulators for Automation of Functional Testing of Long/Short range wireless communication networks including Satellite/Telecom networks and IoT.

My current area of research is at the various intersections of:

- Computational Networks
- Engineering Mathematics
- Network Emulators for Software Testing
- Classic Machine Learning with the tabular quantitative data set.
- Statistics
- Various Programming Languages such as Python, C++/GoLang/Rust, and Java.

I have a proven track record and accomplishments in production-grade software development in Industry and also scientific literature publication in the form of Books, Thesis and Research papers in my area of expertise mentioned.

I am also proud global citizen and published teacher with 15 Books, 3 courses in top ed-tech platforms, open access Blog and open access YouTube channel.

I offer to teach Computational Mathematics, Data Science, ML/DL, Internet of Things, Programming languages, Web technologies, Cloud Computing, Microcontrollers, Electronics for Computer Scientists, Operating Systems, Computer Networks, Data Structures and Algorithms, Software Engineering and Software Testing.

I am not so keen on teaching Automata and Formal Languages to undergraduates but I can teach the same subject to masters students. Also, I can teach formal models in computer science to master students along with the usage and programming of the NuSMV tool.

I am a Life-Long learner with many areas of interests. Earlier, I have worked in Wireless Network Software Organization as Lead Software Engineer for close to a decade. I was in USA for two long stints and was instrumental in

Releases of Mobility Manager at Motorola USA as Single Point of Contact for Network Simulator Tool. My Research is available as Books and Thesis in IJSER, USA. My Thesis published as Book is rated as one of the best Books of all time for Regression testing by BookAuthority.org. I am an Active Researcher in the field of Computational Mathematics, Machine Learning, Deep Learning, Data Science, Artificial Intelligence, Regression Testing applied to Networks, Communication and Internet of Things. I am an active contributor of Science, Technology, Engineering and Mathematics. I am currently working on few Undisclosed Books. I have started Blogging recently on Technology and Allied Areas. I have been National and International awardee. I am Senior IEEE member since 2013 and member of Smart Tribe and Cheeky Scientists Association. I am UGC-NET Qualified (2012). Recipient of several Bravo awards for deserving work at Motorola. I am on the Editorial Board of few Scientific Journals. I am an ardent reader of STEM(Science, Technology, Engineering and Mathematics). I have desire to contribute more to STEM.

I

Mathematics for Computer Scientists and Engineers

Mathematics is a fundamental stepping stone or building block for Science and many other fields of Engineering. Computer Science and Engineering is no exception.

1

Mathematics for Computer Scientists and Engineers

Mathematics is a fundamental stepping stone or building block for Science and many other fields of Engineering. Computer Science and Engineering is no exception.

Let us start with:

1. Mathematical Structures for Computer Science by Judith L. Gersting by W. H. Freeman and Company. This Book is comprehensive and application-oriented. Application of concepts to the real-world problems of computer science
2. Mathematics for Computer Science by Eric Lehman, F Thomson Leighton, and Albert R Meyer. Available LibreTexts.

Noteworthy publications for **additional knowledge** although they are tilted towards other fields of Engineering viz. Electronics, Mechanical, and Civil.

1. Engineering Mathematics by Croft, Davison, Hargreaves, and Flint by Pearson
2. Bird's Comprehensive Engineering Mathematics, John Bird by Routledge.

3. Hand Book of Mathematics by Andrei D. Polyanin and Alexander V. Manzhirov by CRC Press
4. Advanced Engineering Mathematics by Dennis G. Zill by Jones and Bartlett Learning.
5. Many other good Books by prominent Authors

2

Probability and Statistics for Engineers and Scientists

Although Probability and Statistics are dealt with briefly in the Books mentioned in Chapter 1, they deserve Books of their own. Following are noteworthy Books.

1. Introduction to Probability and Statistics for Engineers and Scientists by Sheldon M. Ross published by Elsevier.
2. Applied Statistics and Probability for Engineers by Douglas C. Montgomery and George C. Runger by Wiley.

Both are treasures as they apply concepts to real-world problem definitions. There are many other great Books by other prominent Authors.

II

Electronics for Computer Scientists and Engineers

The study of Medicine and human physiology for that matter is incomplete without the study of human anatomy. With that fundamental preamble let us start this section. We also talk about microcontrollers mainly used Embedded devices. We talk about Analog and Digital Circuits which can be peripheral devices or on their own. We talk about what computer architecture looks like.

3

Analog and Digital Circuits

The following are noteworthy Books. First Book is Electronic Circuits and the Second and Third are for Digital Circuits.

1. Electronics Fundamentals Circuits, Devices and Applications Thomas L. Floyd David L. Buchla by Pearson
2. Digital Electronics Principles, Devices and Applications Anil K. Maini by Wiley
3. Digital Design by M. Morris Mano and Michael D. Ciletti by Pearson

Noteworthy Book which is Practical Oriented:

1. Electronics Cookbook, Practical Electronic Recipes with Arduino and Raspberry Pi by Simon Monk by Oreilly

4

Micro Controllers

Some great resources for Microcontroller and Embedded Systems are:

1. Embedded Systems Volume 1,2,3 by Jonathan W. Valvano
2. Fast and Effective Embedded Systems Design by Rob Toulson Tim Wilmshurst
3. The Definitive Guide to ARM Cortex-M3 and Cortex-M4 Processors Third Edition Joseph Yiu

5

Computer Architecture

Two noteworthy Books are:

1. Computer System Architecture by M. Morris Mano
2. The Architecture of Computer Hardware, System Software & Networking An Information Technology Approach by Irv Englander

III

Programming Languages for Computer Scientists and Engineers

To program the computers, knowledge of programming languages is essential. Programming languages can be classified using various methods. As of now there is no single programming language that can be used for all purposes. However, Python comes close to it.

6

C, C++, GoLang and Rust

The following Languages are most suitable for System Software, Embedded Systems, and Networking.

1. Problem Solving and Program Design in C by Hanley and Koffman by Pearson
2. Modern C++ for Absolute Beginners Slobodan Dmitrović by Apress
3. Beginning C++17 or C++20 Ivor Horton Peter Van Weert by Apress
4. Working draft, Standard for C++ programming language, latest
5. The Rust Programming Language (Covers Rust 2018) Book by Carol Nichols and Steve Klabnik by no Stratch Press
6. Rust by example on line book https://doc.rust lang.org/rust-by-example/
7. Programming Rust Fast, Safe Systems Development Jim Blandy and Jason Orendorff by Oreilly
8. The Go Programming Language Book by Alan A. A. Donovan and Brian Kernighan
9. The way to Go by Ivo Balbaret
10. Introducing Go Build Reliable, Scalable Programs by Caleb Doxsey by Oreilly Press

7

Python, Java, Kotlin, JavaScript, HTML5 and CSS3

The programming languages Python and Java are most suited for application software. While JavaScript, HTML5 and CSS3 are most suited for web programming. Kotlin is most suited for Mobile application development. Although new generation flutter is used for Mobile, Web, and Desktop Applications.

A few noteworthy Books are:

1. Python latest documentation by Team Guido and Python
2. Many great Authoritative Books on Python by great Authors
3. Java for Absolute Beginners by Iuliana Cosmina
4. Java in a Nutshell, Seventh Edition by Ben Evans and David Flanagan
5. Java Program Design Principles, Polymorphism and Patterns by Edward Sciore
6. JavaScript: Novice to Ninja 2nd Edition by Darren Jones
7. HTML5, CSS3 by Flavio by CodeValley.
8. Many other great Books on Java/JavaScript and scripting languages HTML/CSS

IV

Software Engineering

The most prominent field of Computer Science and Engineering with vast Industrial applications is Software Engineering. Software Architecture, Design, and Testing are dominant fields of software engineering.

8

Software Engineering

Two most widely Books are:

1. Software Engineering a practitioner's approach by Pressman and Maxim by McGrawHill
2. Software Engineering by Ian Sommerville by Addison-Wesley

9

Software Architecture and Design

The first three are architecture-related Books. Fourth is a design-related Book.

1. Software Architecture for Developers by Simon Brown
2. Software Architecture in Practice by Len Bass
3. Essential Software Architecture Ian Gorton
4. Design Pattern Books in your Chosen Language Ex. Head First Design Pattern in Java/Python.

10

Software Testing

Some great Books by great Authors in the field of software testing are below which are mostly ISTQB certification oriented. However 6 is mostly Academic treatment of the subject by Wiley publication.

1. Bath, Graham, and Erik van Veenendaal. Improving the Test Process: Implementing Improvement and Change—a Study Guide for the ISTQB Expert Level Module. 1st edition, Rocky Nook Inc, 2014.
2. Guide to Advanced Software Testing by Anne Mette Jonassen Hass published by Artech House
3. Black, Rex, et al. Agile Testing Foundations: An ISTQB Foundation Level Agile Tester Guide. 2017.
4. Black, Rex, and Jamie L. Mitchell. Advanced Software Testing. 1st ed, RockyNook, 2009.
5. FOUNDATIONS OF SOFTWARE TESTING ISTQB CERTIFICATION, 4TH EDITION. CENGAGE LEARNING EMEA, 2019.
6. Naik, Kshirasagar, and Priyadarshi Tripathy. Software Testing and Quality Assurance: Theory and Practice. John Wiley & Sons, 2008.
7. Roman, Adam. The ISTQB Foundation Level 2018 Syllabus: Test Techniques and Sample Exams. 1st edition, Springer Berlin Heidelberg, 2018.
8. Few other great Books by Authoritative Authors

V

Scientific Software

The software that is used for understanding and further exploring Physics, Chemistry, Biology, and their sub-fields and allied fields. Mathematical libraries provided by open source such as Sympy, and Scipy, and tools like Sage, and Matlab are indispensable nowadays for these activities.

11

Scientific Software

The software that is used for understanding and further exploring Physics, Chemistry, Biology, and their sub-fields and allied fields. Mathematical libraries provided by open source such as Sympy, and Scipy, and tools like Sage, and Matlab are indispensable nowadays for these activities.

Few noteworthy references are:

1. Scipy lecture notes latest by many Authors demonstrating the capabilities of library
2. Sympy documentation online by team Sympy for demonstrating the sympy library capabilities
3. Scipy documentation online by team Scipy for demonstrating the Scipy library capabilities
4. Matlab documentation online
5. Few Books by other great Authors

VI

Data Structures and Algorithm

Depending upon the need of situation we store the data in built in or custom structures of data such as array, linked list and we operate on them using various Algorithms to perform certain operations such as sorting and searching.

12

Data Structures and Algorithms

Depending upon the need of the situation we store the data in built-in or custom structures of data such as array, and linked list and we operate on them using various Algorithms to perform certain operations such as sorting and searching. A few note-worthy Books are listed below. Book 1 is the starting point.

1. Problem Solving in Data Structures & Algorithms Using C By Hemant Jain Independently published. The reader can start with this. The author also has Books on the same subject in many popular programming languages with GitHub
2. Data Structures & Algorithms in Java by Robert Lafore by SAMS publication. Java Specific.
3. Data Structures and Algorithms in JavaTM/Python by Michael T. Goodrich, Roberto Tamassia, and Michael H. Goldwasser published by Wiley. This Book can be after getting a good grasp of Book 1.

VII

Computer Networking

Computer Network is the core subject of Computer Science and Engineering. Essentially we talk about the interconnection of many computationally capable networks connected to each other by various protocols.

13

Computer Networking

Computer Network is the core subject of Computer Science and Engineering. Essentially we talk about the interconnection of many computationally capable networks connected to each other by various protocols.

1. Computer Networks by Tanenbaum and Wetherall can be great starting point

VIII

Operating System

Operating System is a software that brings complex hardware circuitry to life starting from power on, also provides various system software interfaces such as file editor, compiler, linker, loader, and file copy interfaces. It also does scheduling, power management, etc to name a few. In bare metal systems, an operating system may be missing altogether. A few examples are Desktop operating systems such as Windows, Linux, and Mac. Ubuntu, Red Hat Enterprise Linux for servers. Various RTOSes.

14

Operating System

Operating System is a software that brings complex hardware circuitry to life starting from power on, also provides various system software interfaces such as file editor, compiler, linker, loader, and file copy interfaces. It also does scheduling, power management, etc to name a few. In bare metal systems, an operating system may be missing altogether. A few examples are Desktop operating systems such as Windows, Linux, and Mac. Ubuntu, Red Hat Enterprise Linux for servers. Various RTOSes such as Real Time Linux. Or it could be Contiki for very resource-constrained field devices. Or it could be distributed OS.

A few starting point Books are:

1. Minix Operating System Design and Implementation by Andrew Tenenbaum and Woodhull. There is a source code in the index allowing the reader to study the implementation part.

A few other noteworthy Books are:

1. Operating Systems Concepts by Abraham Silberschatz, Peter B. Galvin, and Greg Gagne
2. Operating systems by Gary Nutt, Nabendu Chaki, and Sarmisth Neogy.

IX

Finite Automata, Formal Languages and Logic in Computer Science

Both deterministic and non deterministic finite state automata, formal languages for unambiguos specifications and logic in computer science are essential for Computer Science and Engineering with their own formal notations and their meaning.

15

Finite Automata, Formal Languages and Logic in Computer Science

Both deterministic and nondeterministic finite state automata, formal languages for unambiguous specifications, and logic in computer science are essential for Computer Science and Engineering with their own formal notations and their meaning.

A few noteworthy Books are:

1. An introduction to formal languages and automata by Peter Linz.
2. Logic in Computer Science, Modelling and Reasoning about Systems by Michael Huth and Mark Ryan by Cambridge University Press and solution manual accompanying this Book

A tool of particular interest is:

1. NuSMV or New Symbolic Model Verifier open source tool. It's manual and user guide. It is a Tool by CMU, FBK-irst. and ITC-irst.

Reference Book:

1. Using Z Specification, Refinement, and Proof by Jim Woodcock and Jim Davies, University of Oxford

X

Utilities for Computer Scientists and Engineers

Utilities help in compiling, linking, linting, code formatting, memory leak checking, version control, debugging etc for production grade software are utilities. In modern days powerful Integrated Development Environments are one stop solution for all these activities. Examples include VSCode along with it extensions, IntelliJ for Java, Pycharm for Python to name a few.

XI

Web Technologies

Web technology study involves the study of a combination of Front End, Back End, and Libraries to write to databases, and deployment environment to name a few.

16

Web Technologies

This is a very vast topic. People use JavaScript for the front end(Angular, React, Vue). Java(Spring boot), Python (Flask, Django), Rust, JavaScript, Golang as server-side programming. Plus various databases such as SQL and NoSQL. And their various permutation and combinations.

Developers develop mobile applications using various implementation languages such as Kotlin on Android. The applications could be Native, Web, or Hybrid. There is a new movement to use the Flutter platform. Which promises the same code base for Mobile(Android and iOS), Web, and Desktop.

Then there is no code/ low code motion by Bubble, Joget, Kissflow, or Wordpress. Have a look at the following links:

1. https://www.simbla.com/
2. https://www.wix.com
3. https://thunkable.com
4. https://vaadin.com/designer
5. https://bootstrapstudio.io/

Many many more.

Some noteworthy Online Teachers FrontEnd+Backend

ESSENTIAL KNOWLEDGE FOR COMPUTER SCIENTISTS AND ENGINEERS

1. Angela Yu
2. Trevor Sawler
3. Andrew Mead
4. John Purcell
5. In 28 Minutes by Ranga
6. Academind by Maximilian
7. Jose Salviterra

There are Books in higher triple digits.

XII

Data Bases

Databases Bases is where data is stored persistently and securely. Kind of warehouse for Data. Database management software helps in managing this data mentioned earlier.

17

Data bases

Databases is where data is stored persistently and securely. Database management software helps in managing this data mentioned earlier.

1. Database Systems A Pragmatic Approach Elvis C. Foster With Shripad Godbole by Apress
2. Database System Concepts Seventh Edition by Avi Silberschatz, Henry F. Korth, and S. Sudarshan.

For particular flavors of relational databases such as PostgreSQL, MySQL, MSSQL, or NoSQL such as MongoDB you could refer to respective books. I particularly find the following to-the-point tutorials from TutorialsPoint very convenient for "introductory" concepts:

1. SQL TUTORIAL Simply Easy Learning by tutorialspoint.com
2. Similar material you should be able to find for MongoDB and others.

XIII

Productivity Software Such as Office Suites

For example, to communicate your research findings you need a good word processor software that supports intense mathematical expression, etc. Plus it should not drain too much of your productive hours as the intention is content creation and not content creation software usage expertise.

18

Productivity Software

For example, to communicate your research findings you need a good word processor software that supports intense mathematical expression, etc. Plus it should not drain too much of your productive hours as the intention is content creation and not content creation software usage expertise.

Example LibreOffice and Microsoft Office suite of Tools. LibreOffice comes with Writer, Draw, Impress(Presentation), and Calc(Spreadsheet). Similarly, Microsoft offers Word, Excel, and PowerPoint. For writing, some organizations may be using old word processors such as Latex in such cases you could use Lyx which is what you see as what you get an editor. Still, better you could use Reedsy for Book writing. For Mathematics intensive content Mathcha editor is an excellent choice. Of late lot of support is provided in Microsoft Word thus scientific and research community is not forced to use Tex/Latex. Katex and MathJax need particular mention for Math content.

Case study:

Typora + MathJax, Mathcha editor, and MSWord are making Mathematics Academic writing fun.

Also, **markdown** has come such a long way. Create a Book in Typora with a markdown and see yourself.

XIV

Artificial Intelligence

Machine Learning, Deep Learning, Natural Language Processing, Reinforcement Learning, and General Artificial Intelligence to name a few are sub-fields of Artificial Intelligence. This fie;d is vast and boundaryless. As of 2023 still lot of research is happening. Especially in the field of Artificial General Intelligence or Deep Artificial Intelligence.

19

Artificial Intelligence

Machine Learning, Deep Learning, Natural Language Processing, Reinforcement Learning, and General Artificial Intelligence to name a few are subfields of Artificial Intelligence. This fie;d is vast and boundaryless. As of 2023 still lot of research is happening. Especially in the field of Artificial General Intelligence or Deep Artificial Intelligence.

1. Artificial Intelligence A Modern Approach by Stuart Russell and Peter Norvig by Prentice Hall (Pearson)

The popularity of this speaks volumes.

20

Machine Learning and Deep Learning

You could start learning Machine Learning and Deep Learning with online courses including Udemy A-Z courses on Machine Learning and Deep Learning by Super Data Science or by 365 Data Science.. As reference books, you could have

1. Hands-On Machine Learning with Scikit–Learn and TensorFlow by Aurelian Geron
2. Python Machine Learning By Sebastian Raschka, Vahid Mirjalili
3. The Hundred Page Machine Learning by Burkov
4. Introduction to Machine Learning by Alex Smola and Vishwanathan
5. Deep Learning by Ian, Yoshua, and Aaron
6. Mastering Machine Learning with Python in Six Steps by Manohar-Swamynathan

Some of the machine-learning packages include

1. Scikit learn
2. Keras+Tensorflow
3. JASP and Orange3 for visual programming

For a Mathematics background, you can refer

1. Mathematics for Machine Learning book (Book by A. Aldo Faisal, Cheng Soon Ong, and Marc Peter Deisenroth).

Many good courses in Udemy for Machine Learning and Deep Learning.

21

Natural Language Processing

Natural Language Processing deals with Natural Languages. The language that we humans use for communicating. Say English.

You could start your journey with

1. Natural Language Processing Recipes by Akshay Kulkarni and Adarsha Shivananda by Apress.

22

Re-Inforcement Learning.

In Re-Inforcement Learning we talk about Agents, Environments (And Sensors + Actuators), and Rewards among other things. The journey can start with the following Book.

1. Reinforcement Learning by Abhishek Nandy and Manisha Biswas by Apress

23

Few Good Teachers of Practical AI/ML/DL/RL

Few Noteworthy Teachers with Video/Text Content on the Internet.

- Hadelin de Ponteves
- Kirill Eremenko
- Jose Portilla
- Ryan Ahemad
- Sebastian Raschka
- Micahel Kroeker
- Fabio Nelli
- Aurélien Géron
- Davy, Arno and Mohamed
- ManoharSwamynathan
- Jojo Moolayil
- 365 Careers Team
- Francois Chollet
- Many many more....

XV

Data Science

Data Science is concerned with storage, retrieval, analytics and ultimately inference. Machine Learning and Deep Learning may or may not be part of the Data Science workflow. Data may be structured or unstructured. Data Engineering is part of Data Science.

24

Data Analytics and Data Science

While Data Analytics is analyzing the data, Data Science comprises Data Engineering. and "mostly" Machine Learning and Deep Learning.

1. Python Data Analytics With Pandas, NumPy,and Matplotlib Second Edition Fabio Nelli
2. Python Data Science Handbook by Jake VanderPlas
3. Data Science from Scratch by Joel Grus
4. Python for Data Analysis by Wes McKinney
5. Introducing Data Science big data, machine learning,and more, using python tools by Davy Cielen, Arno d. b. Meysman, Mohamed Ali

XVI

Digital Transformation Technologies

Digital transformation technologies comprises of Cloud, (I) IoT, AI, Block Chain, Security and Communication Technologies. Industry 4.0 is a special/specific case study of application of Digital Transformation.

25

Digital Transformation Technologies

Digital transformation technologies comprises of Cloud, (I) IoT, AI, Block Chain, Security and Communication Technologies. Industry 4.0 is a special/specific case study of application of Digital Transformation.

Cloud:

Talking in particular about AWS there are courses for various levels:

1. AWS Cloud Practitioner
2. AWS Developer
3. AWS Certified Solutions Architect
4. AWS SysOps Administrator

For example on Udemy you can take courses which are aligned for them. For example I have taken AWS Certified (Solutions Architect, Developer, SysOps Administrator, Cloud Practitioner) which is four in one course. Few noteworthy documents follow:

1. AWS General Reference, Reference Guide, https://docs.aws.amazon.com/general/latest/gr/aws-general.pdf

2. Fundamentals of Azure, Microsoft Azure essentials available at Microsoft
3. https://cloud.google.com/docs/overview for Google Cloud

Some great online Teachers

1. BackSpace Academy by Paul Coady
2. Memi Lavi

(I)IoT:

Industrial Intenet of Things is special case of Internet of Things.
For introduction to IoT you could refer:

1. The Intenet of Things: Do it yourself projects by Donald Norris
2. Intenet of Things (IoT) Technologies, Applications, Challenges, and Solutions CRC Press
3. Internet-of-Things (IoT) Systems by Dimitrios Serpanos and Marilyn Wolf
4. Internet of Things: A Hands-on Approach Book by Arshdeep Bahga and Vijay K. Madisetti

For support of IoT in cloud one can refer respective cloud service provider documents:

1. https://azure.microsoft.com/en-in/solutions/architecture/azure-iot-subsystems/
2. AWS IoT Developers Guide available at AWS

AI:

We have already discussed

Block Chain:

Following book can be referred:

1. Blockchain Enabled Applications by Vikram Dhillon David Metcalf Max Hooper
2. BlockChain Revolution by Don Tapscott
3. Hands-On Blockchain with Hyperledger Nitin Gaur Luc Desrosiers Venkatraman Ramakrishna et al.
4. Mastering Bitcoin Programming the Open Blockchain Andreas M. Antonopoulos
5. Blockchain Applications: A Hands-On Approach by Arshdeep Bagha and Vijay Madisetti

Some great teachers online for Block Chain:

1. Kirill Eremenko
2. Hadelin de Pontevas

Communication Technologies:

Can be ZigBee, WiFi, WiMax, Telecom/Satellite Communication.

Some great teachers online for Telecom

1. SatishKumar Jagadeeshan

Security:

Open topic with various types of threats and countermeasures.
   The following two Books should give some feel for various types of threats.

   1. Hacking. Computer hacking, security testing, penetration testing, and Basic Security by Gary Hall and Erin Watson
   2. Mastering Kali Linux for Web Penetration Testing by Michael McPhee

XVII

Quantum Computing

Certain families of Algorithms and practical challenges cannot be solved using Classic Computers. Quantum Computers come to the rescue for such a family of Algorithms. This section is dedicated to Quantum Computing.

26

Quantum Computing

As mentioned earlier, there are few algorithms and practical challenges that can only be solved by Quantum Computers. Is a very niche field with few players as of now:

1. Practical Quantum Computing for Developers by Vladimir Silva by Apress
2. Quantum Computation and Quantum Information by Michael A. Nielsen & Isaac L. Chuang Cambridge University Press
3. Quantum computing for computer scientists Noson S. Yanofsky and Mirco A. Mannucci by Cambridge University Press
4. Quantum Computing for Programmers by Robert Hundt Cambridge University Press

Some good online courses

1. Quantum Computing & Intro to Quantum Machine Learning by Kumaresan Ramanathan

XVIII

Sun Rise Sectors and Role of Computer Scientists and Engineers in Sun Rise Sectors

Sun Rise Sectors are where there will be significant work

27

Sunrise Sectors

Sun Rise Sectors are where there will be significant work. Predicting tech shifts in the coming years is always difficult; **Here are my Big 5 where computer scientists and Engineers will have a role to play.**

- Renewable Energy
- Digital Transformative Technologies
- Cooling Technology
- Private investment in Aerospace Sectors
- Private Investment in Defense Sectors

All these sectors are STEM-dependent. M as in Mathematics. Which means reskilling or upskilling the tech workforce.

XIX

Robotics

Broadly speaking, Robotics is intersection of Mechanical Engineering, Electronics Engineering and Computing.

28

Robotics

Broadly speaking, Robotics is the intersection of Mechanical Engineering, Electronics Engineering, and Computing.

To give the feel of Robotics:

1. Beginning Robotics with Raspberry Pi and Arduino Using Python and OpenCV Jeff Cicolani

XX

Security

Open topic with open threats. We have already briefly touched this topic as a part of Digital Transformation section.

XXI

Reference Material

YouTube, Wikipedia, Libre Project, Chat GPT, GitHub for concrete implementations, LinkedIn Groups, Daily Newsletters, Paid learning platforms such as Udemy, Stack Overflow, Academia.edu, ResearchGate, GeeksForGeeks, and other topic-specific reference materials such as Medium.com.

XXII

Non Technical Knowledge aka. Intangible Traits

Intangible skills include but not limited to Intelligence Quotient, Emotional Quotient, Language Proficiency, Communication skills, Aptitude and Attitude, Team membership and most importantly Ethics and Integrity

Conclusion

www.ingramcontent.com/pod-product-compliance
Lightning Source LLC
Chambersburg PA
CBHW071409220526
45469CB00004B/1217